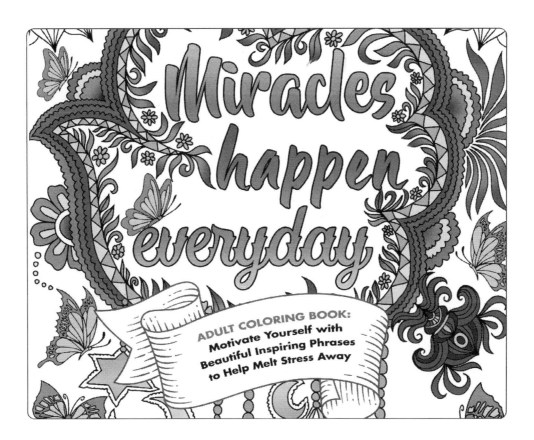

Miracles happen everyday

ADULT COLORING BOOK: Motivate Yourself with Beautiful Inspiring Phrases to Help Melt Stress Away

Copyright 2018 © Coloring Book Cafe

All Rights Reserved.

PUBLISHED BY THE FRUITFUL MIND LTD.

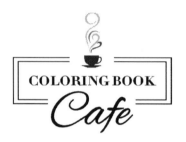

Disclaimer

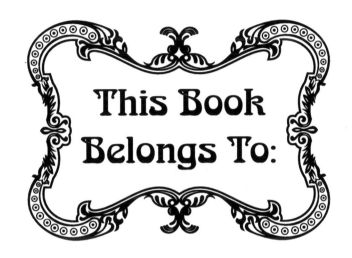

This Book
Belongs To:

BONUS

Relax And Create Your Own Masterpiece With

THIS 30 PAGE FREE *Beautiful Adult Coloring Book*

Claim Your FREE Coloring Book at:

www.freecoloringbooklet.com

Samples Below

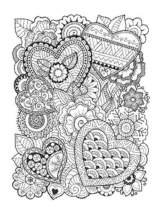 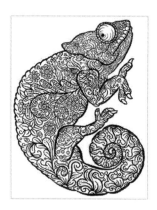 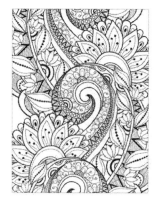

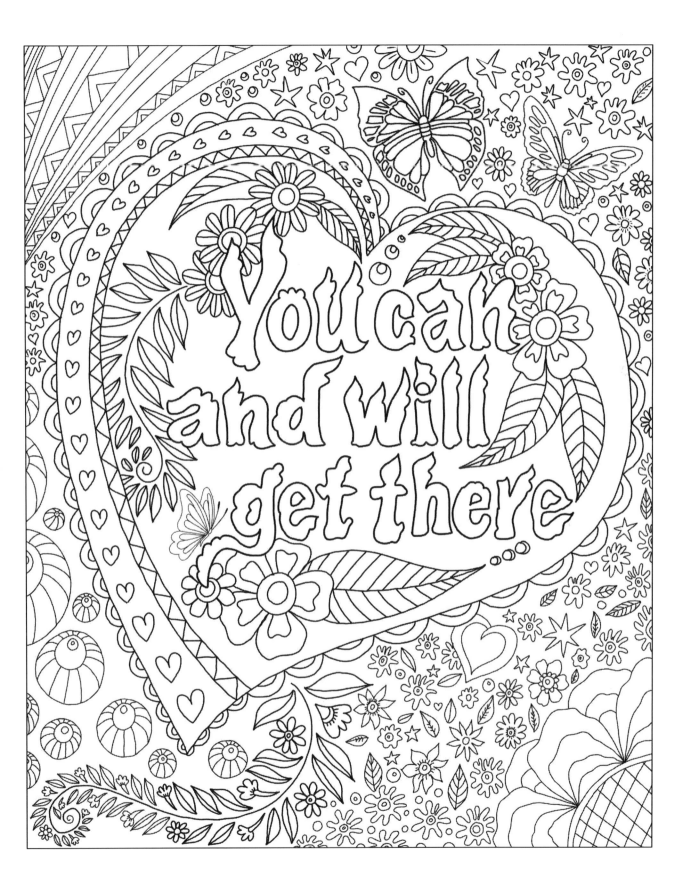

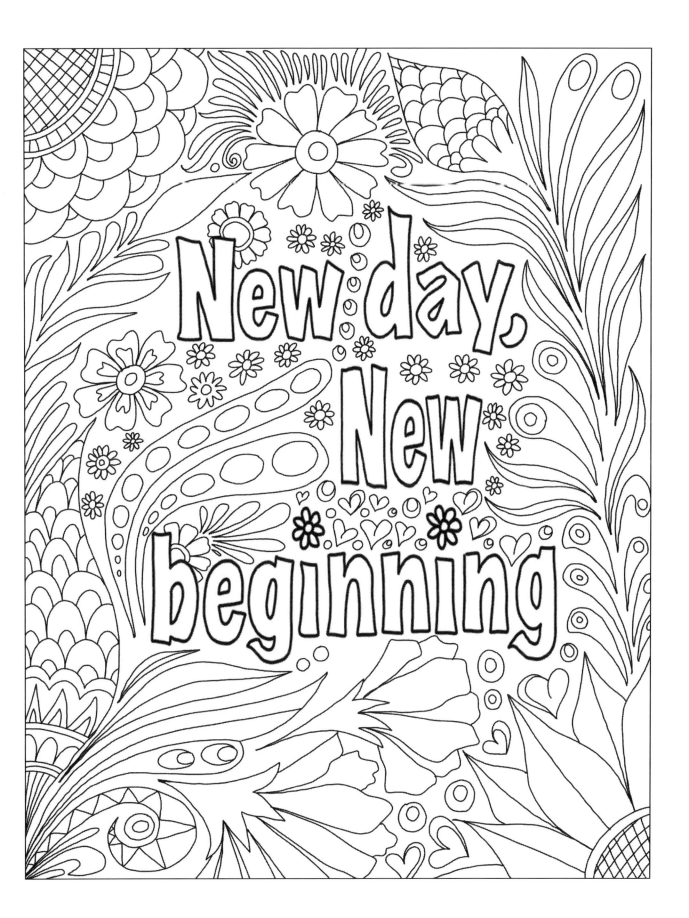

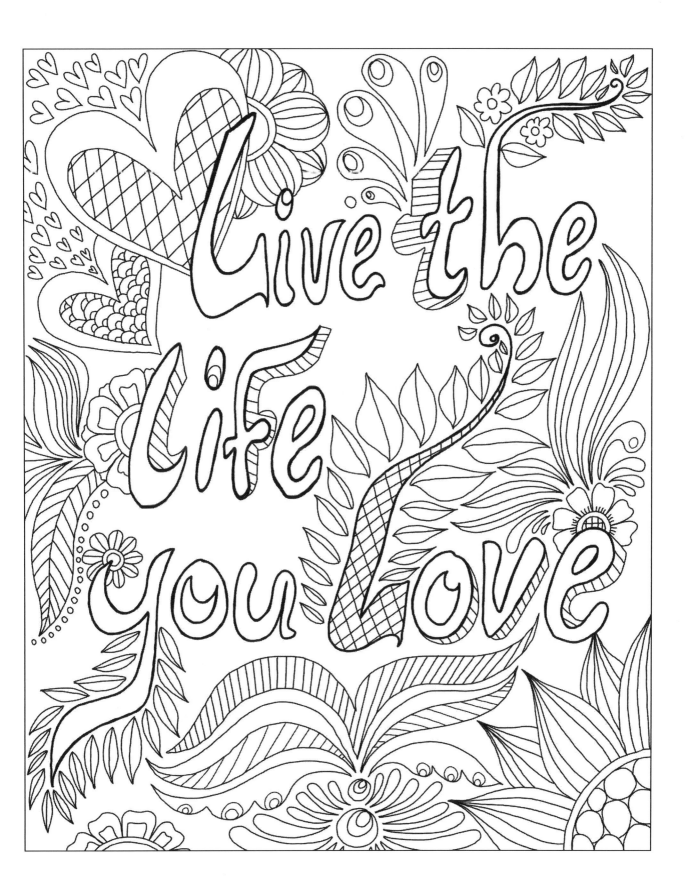

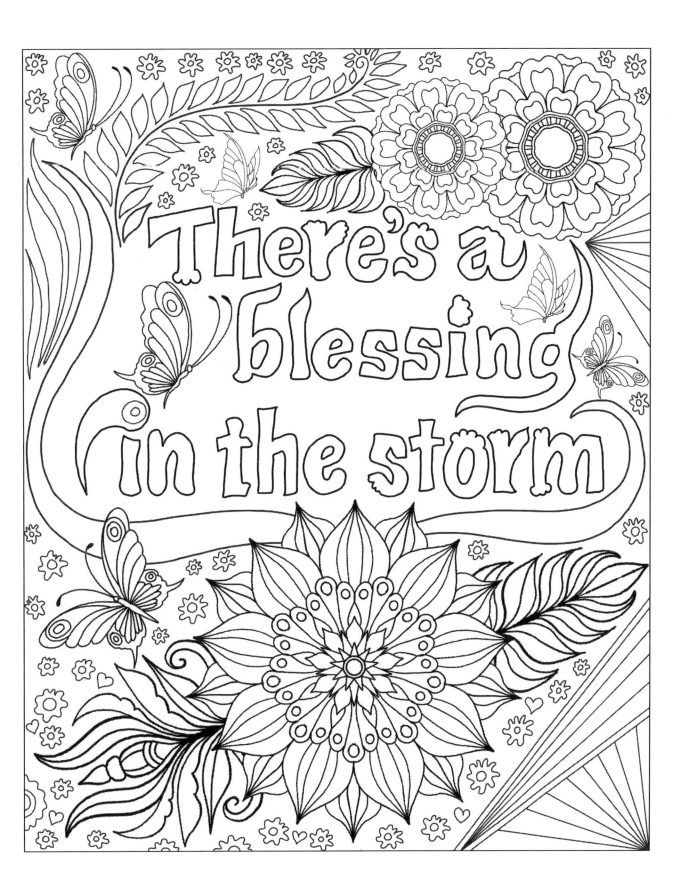

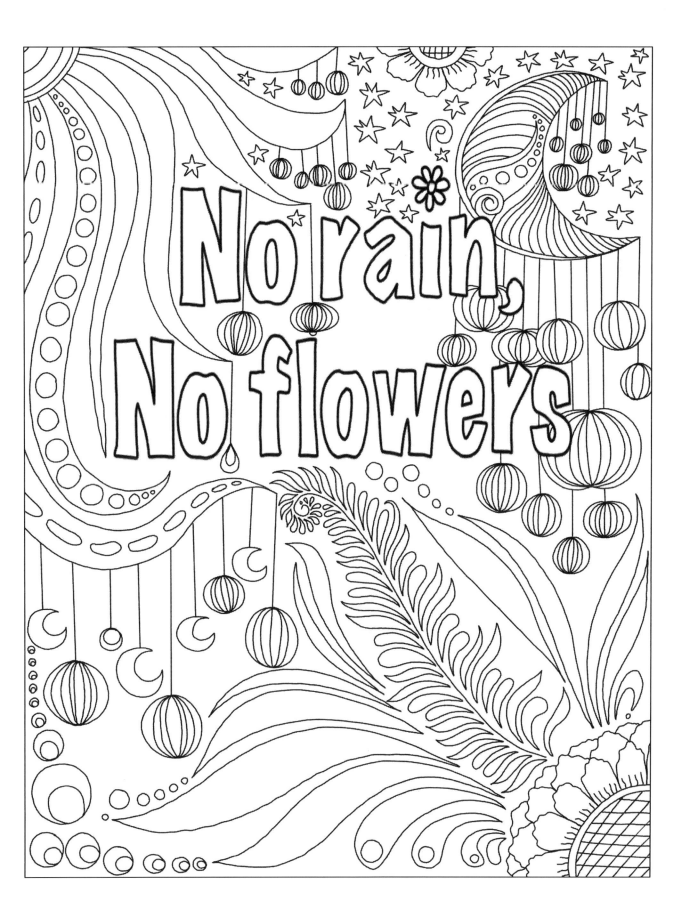

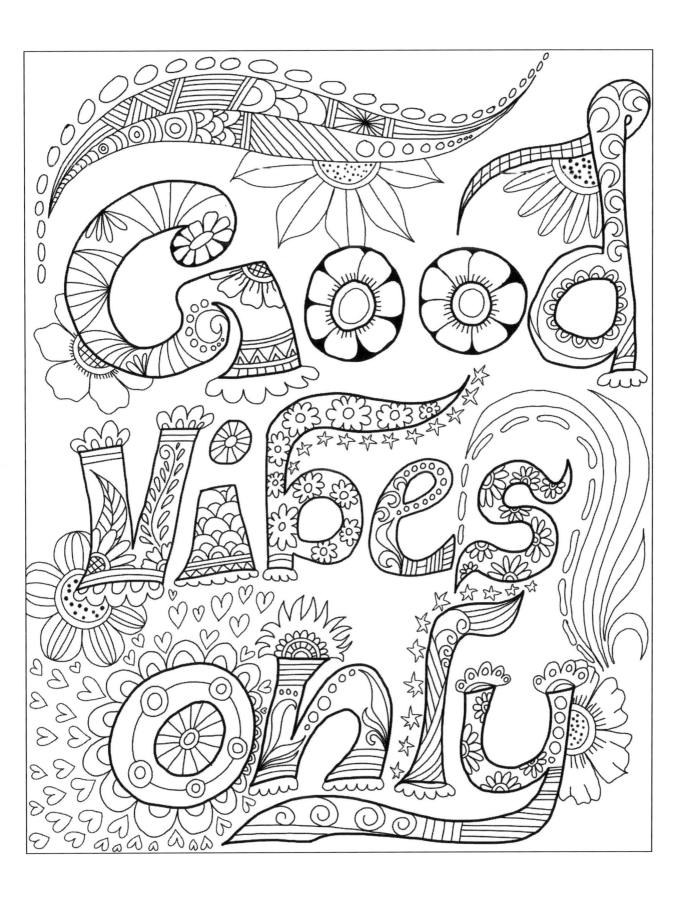

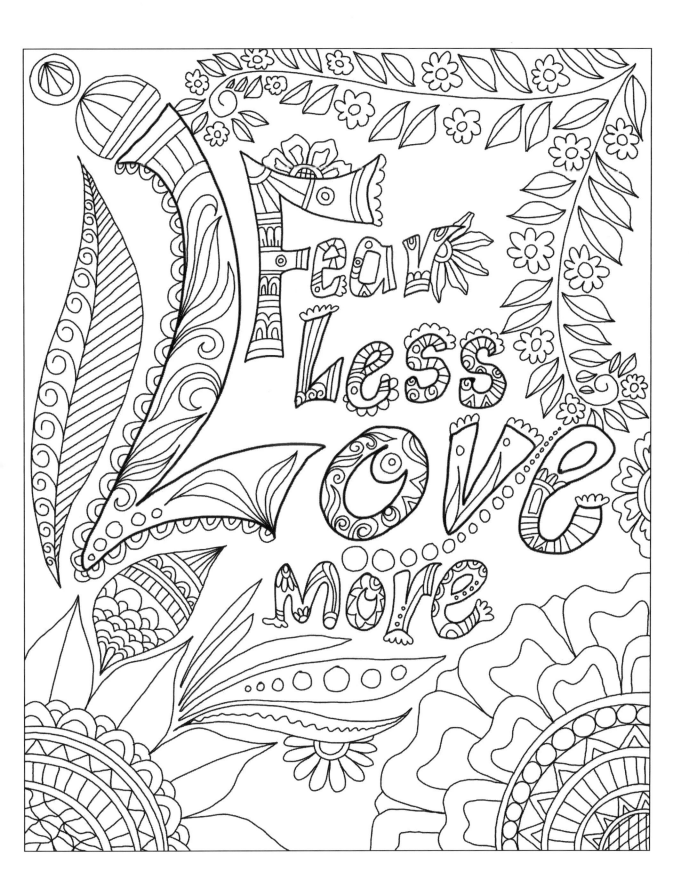

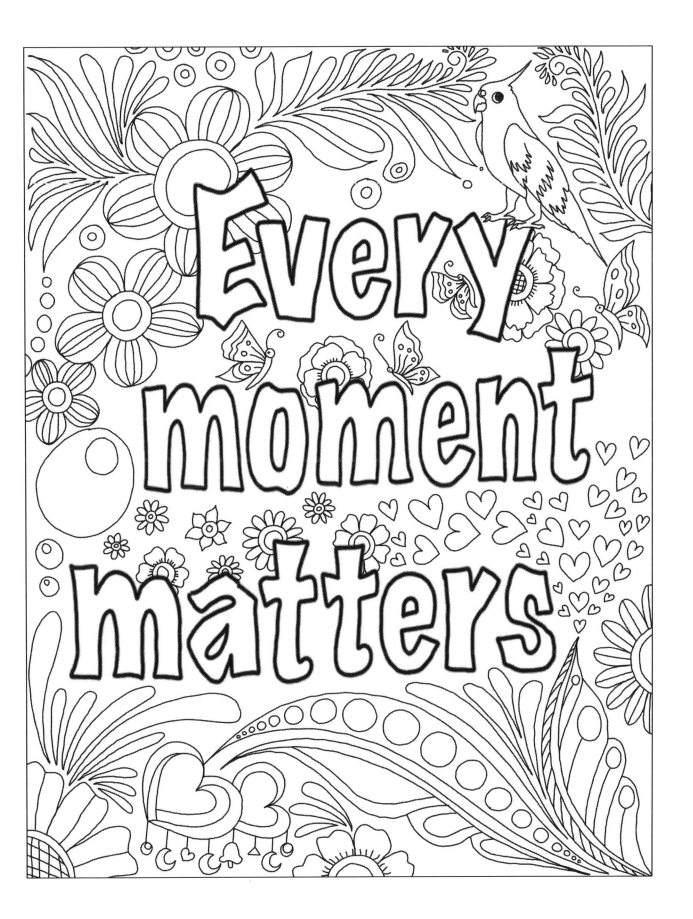

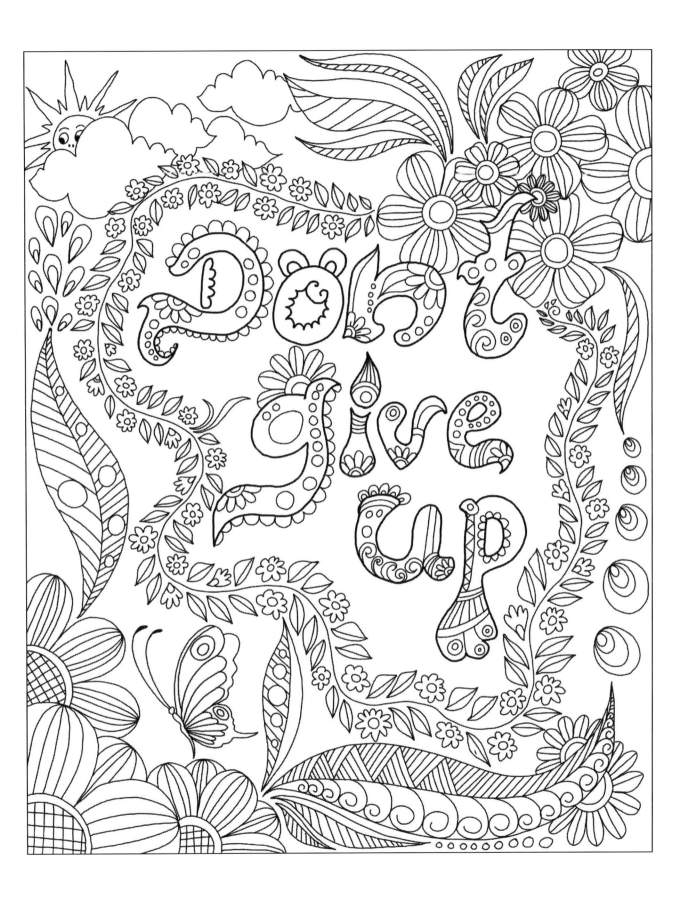

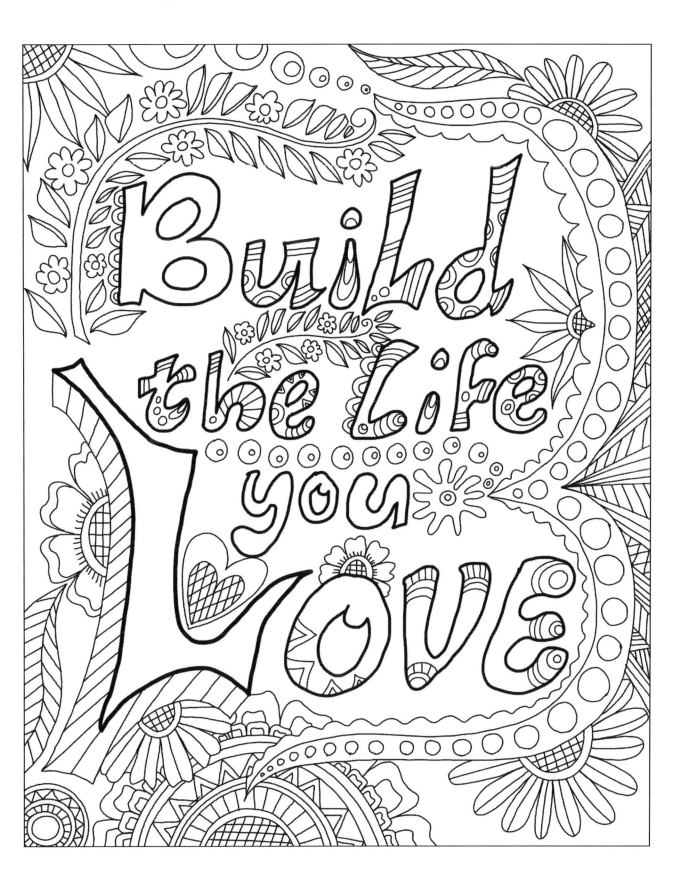

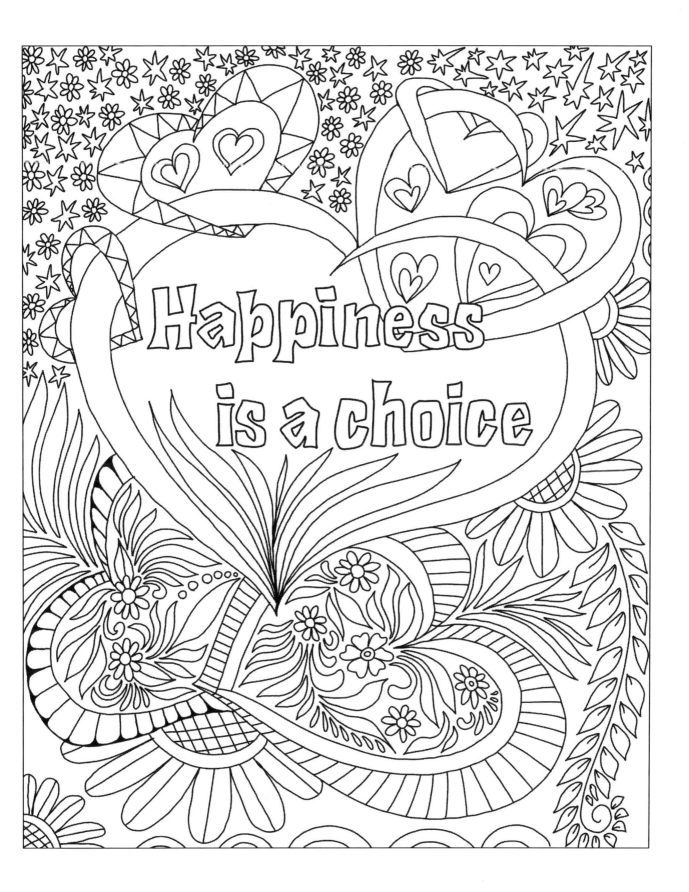

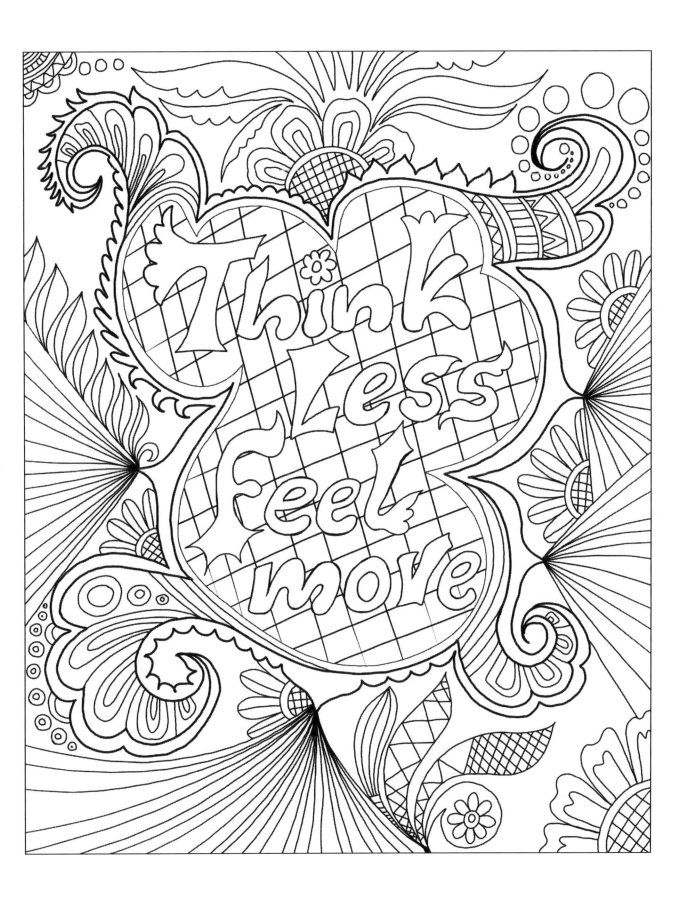

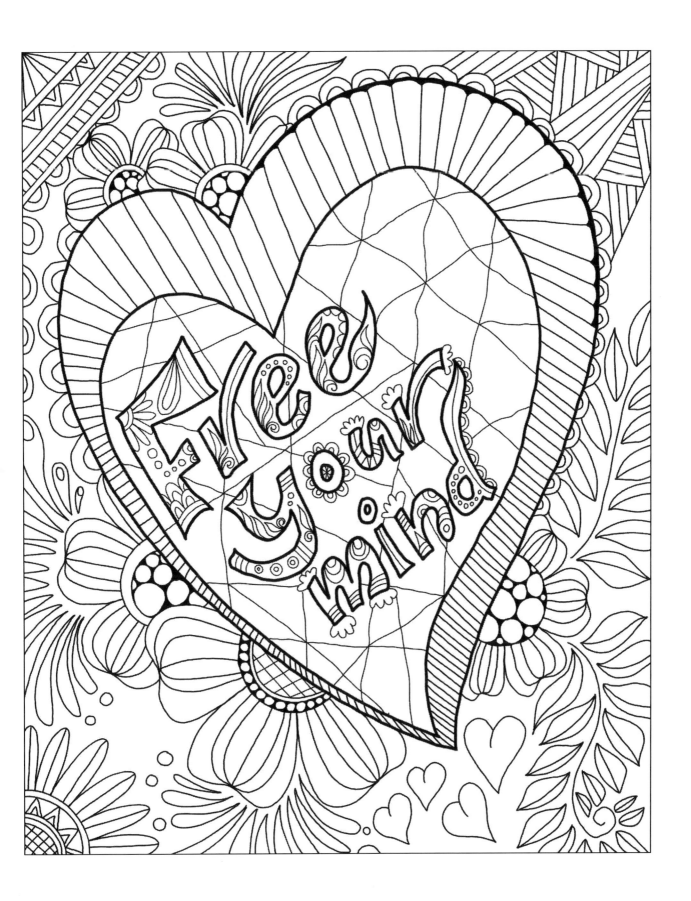

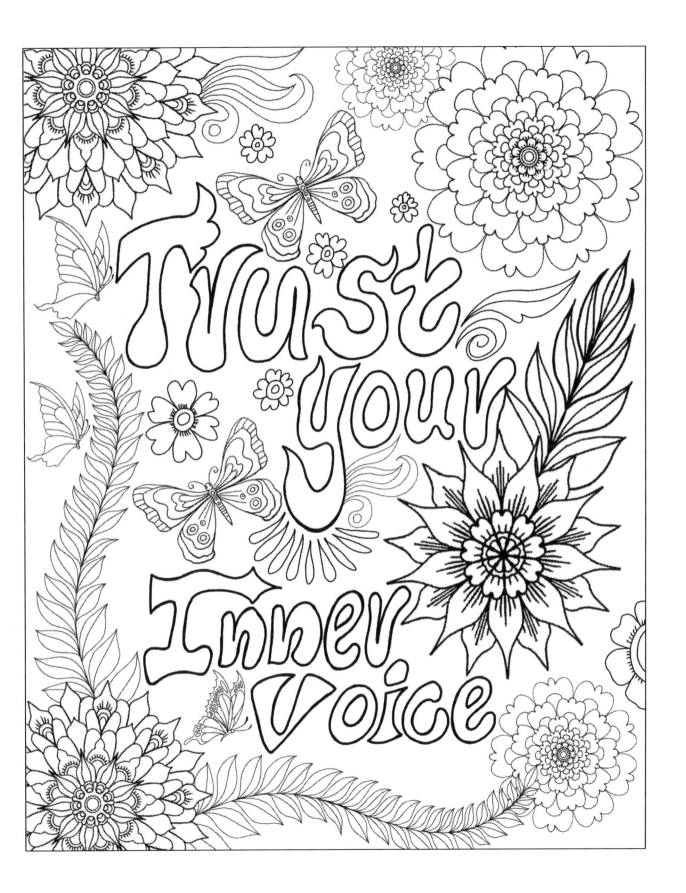

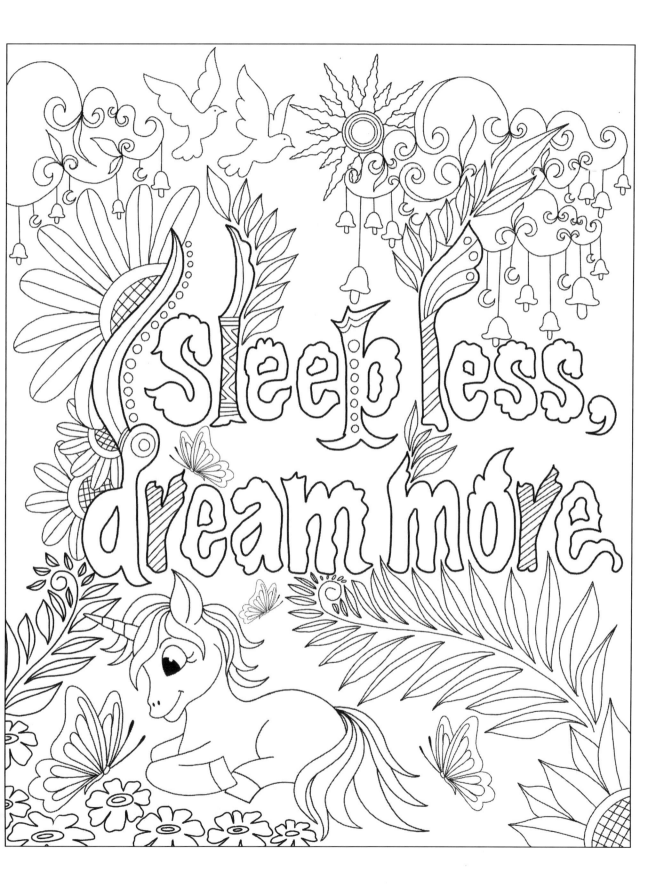

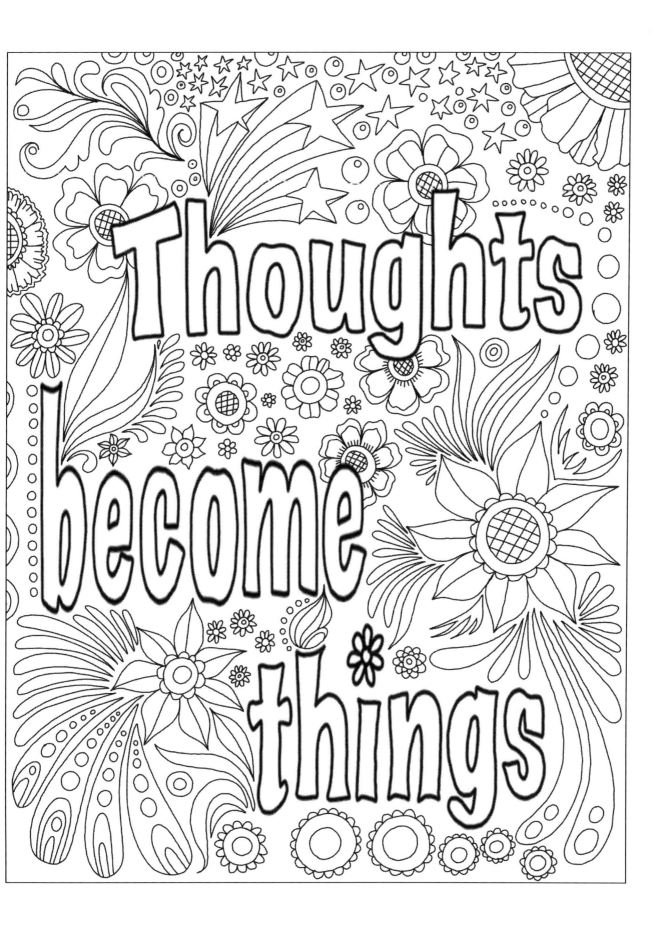

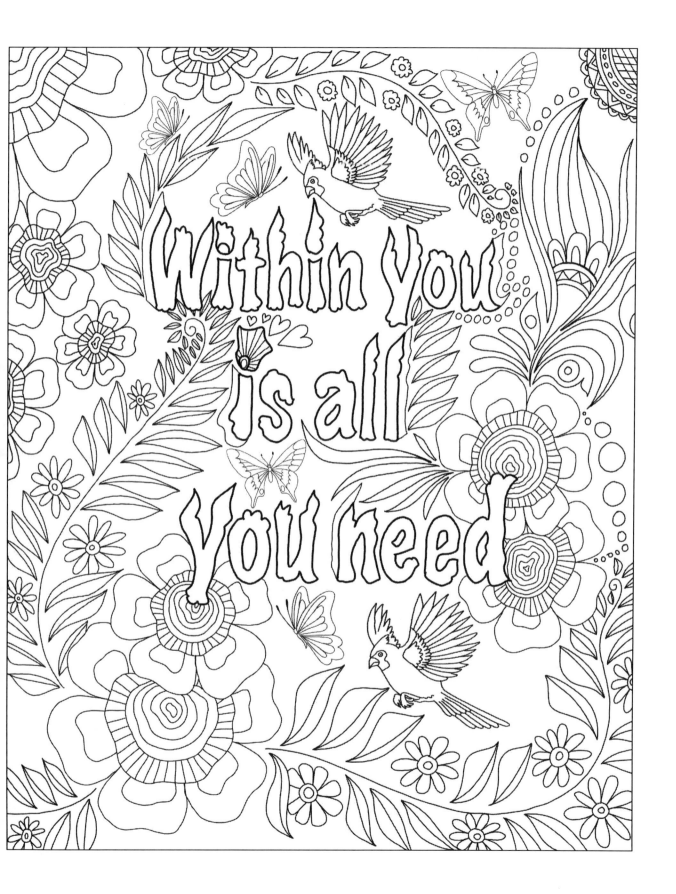

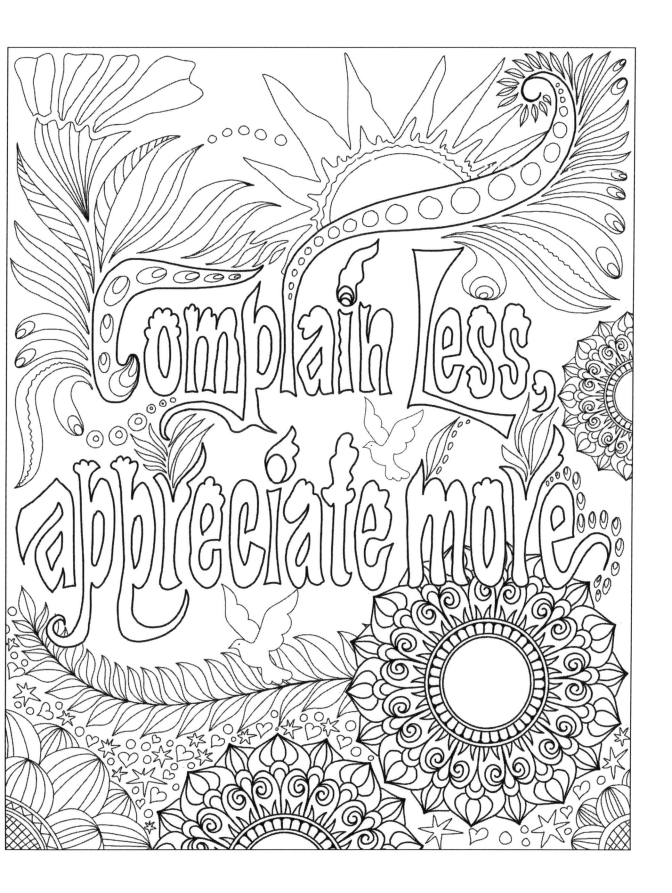

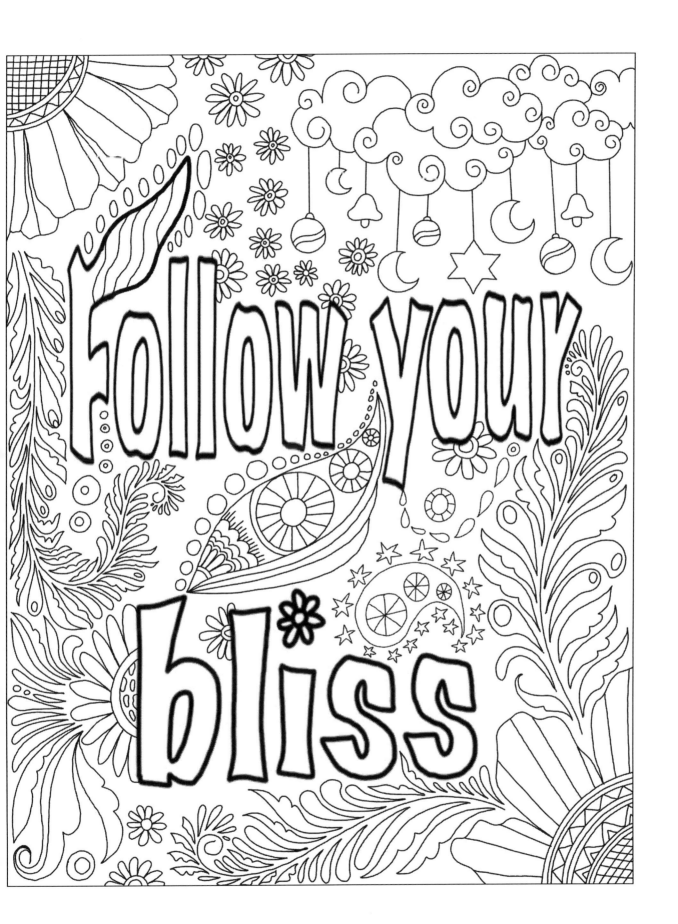

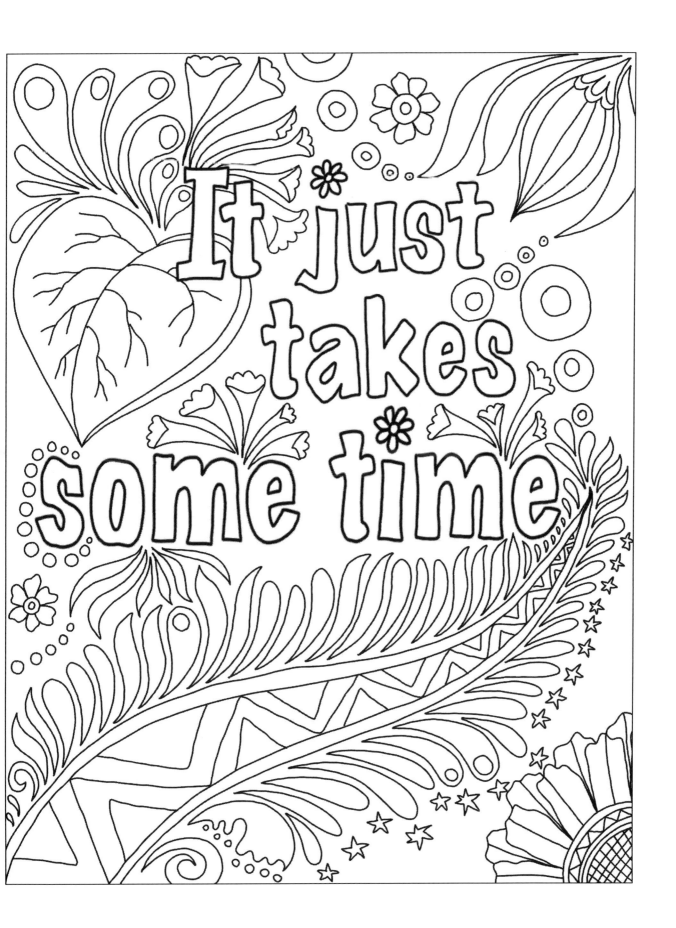

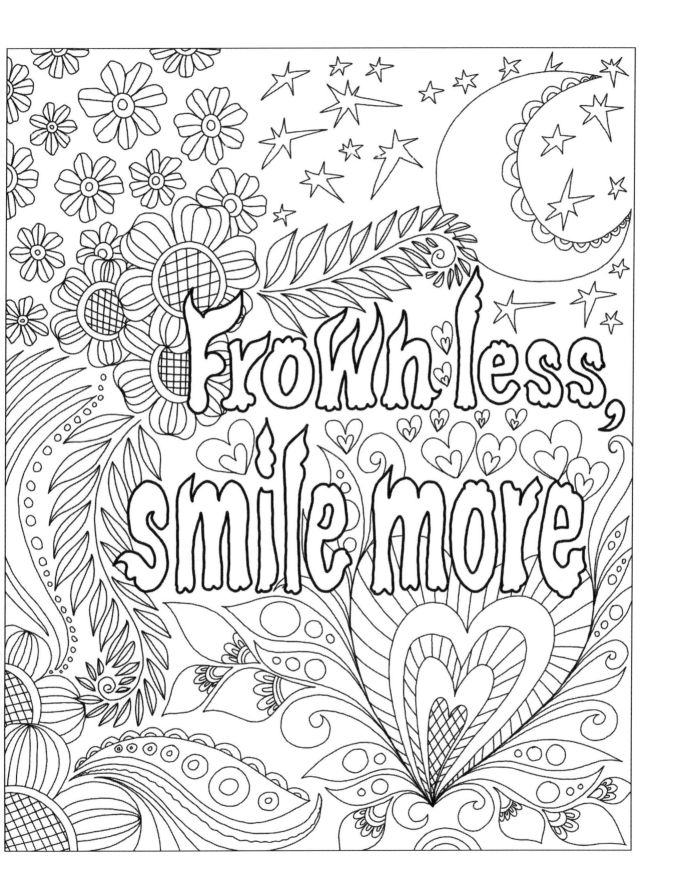

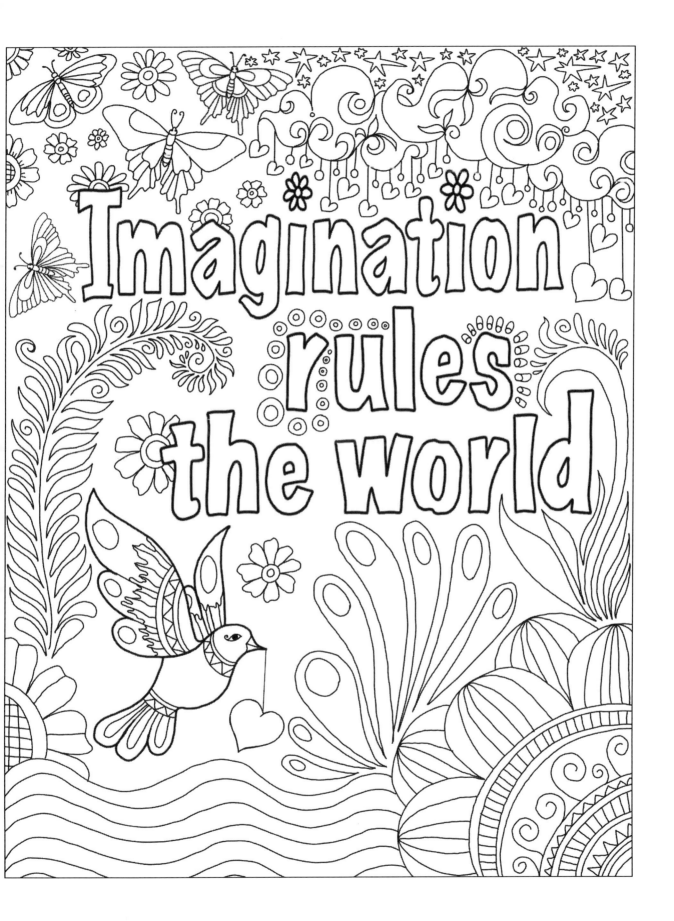

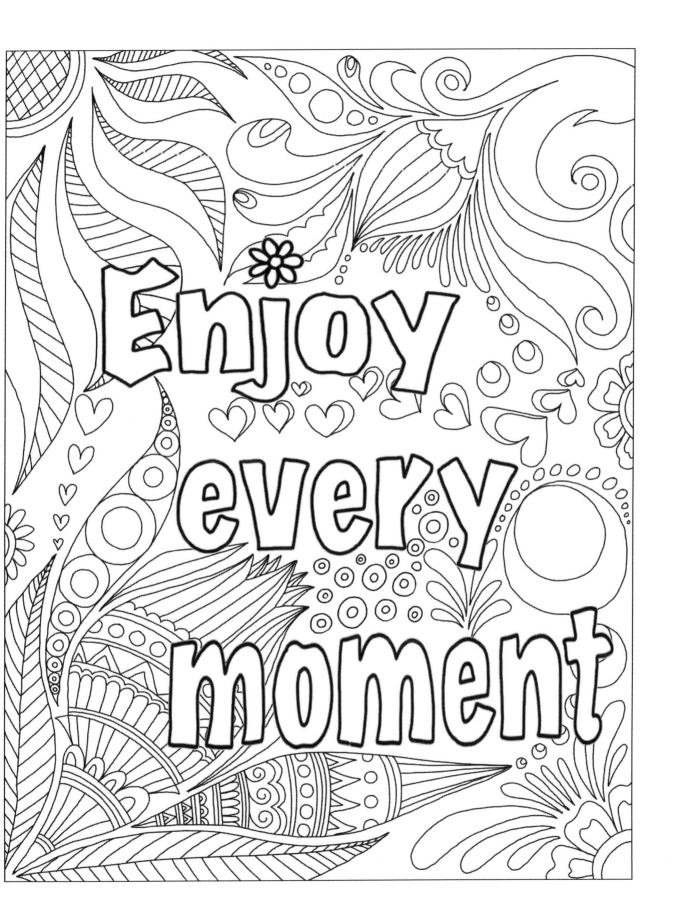

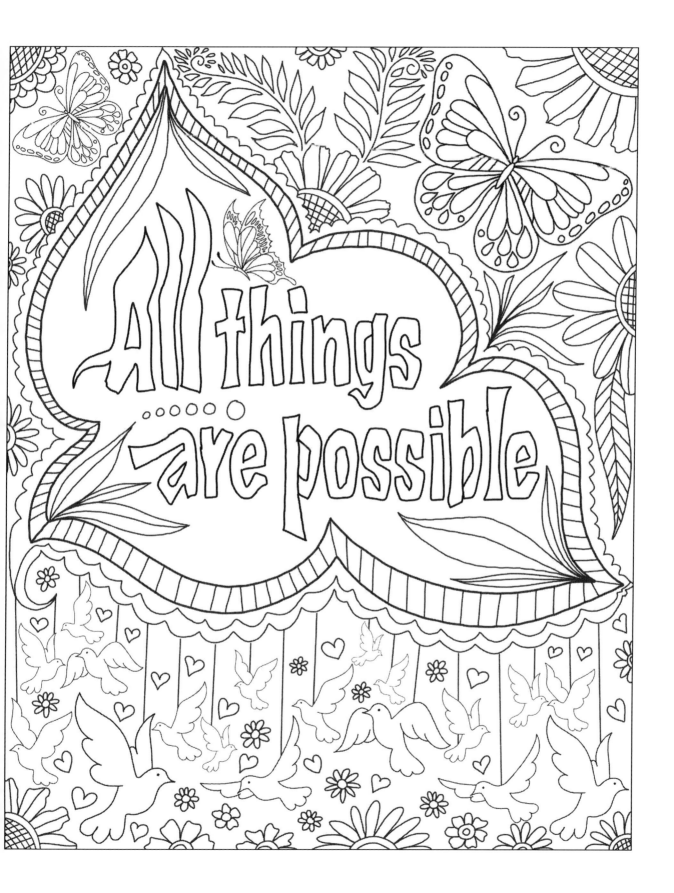

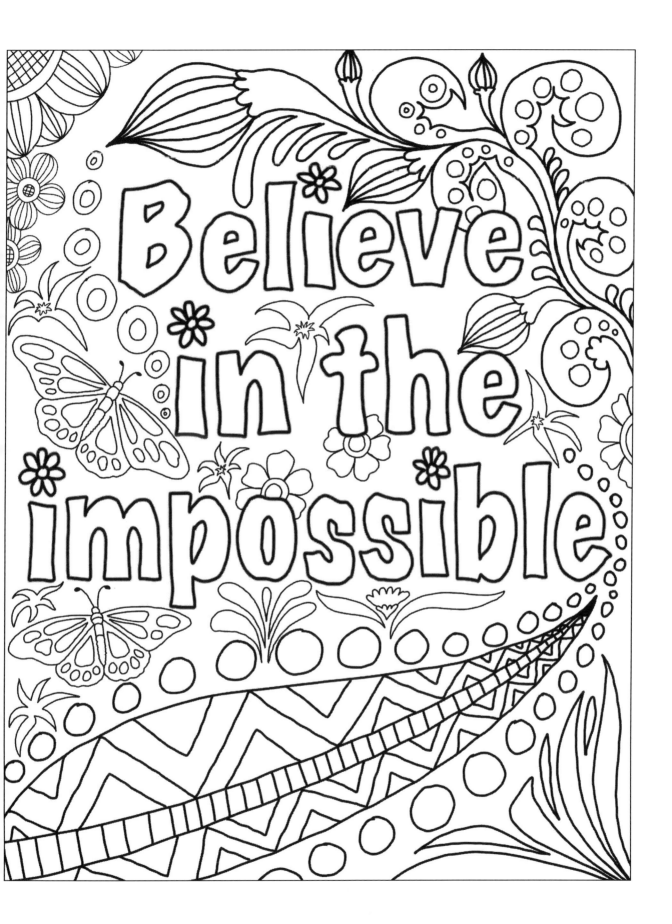

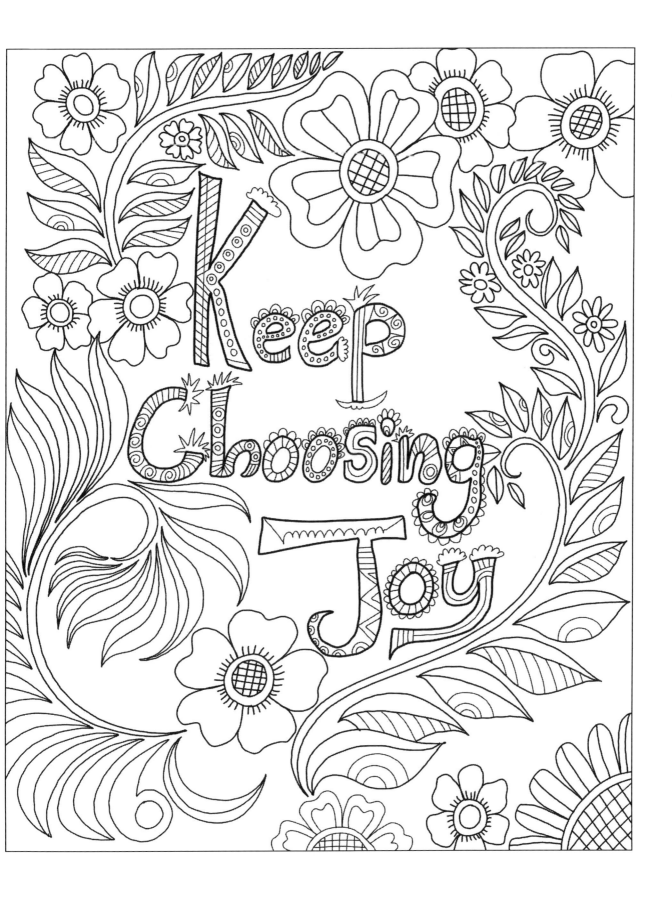

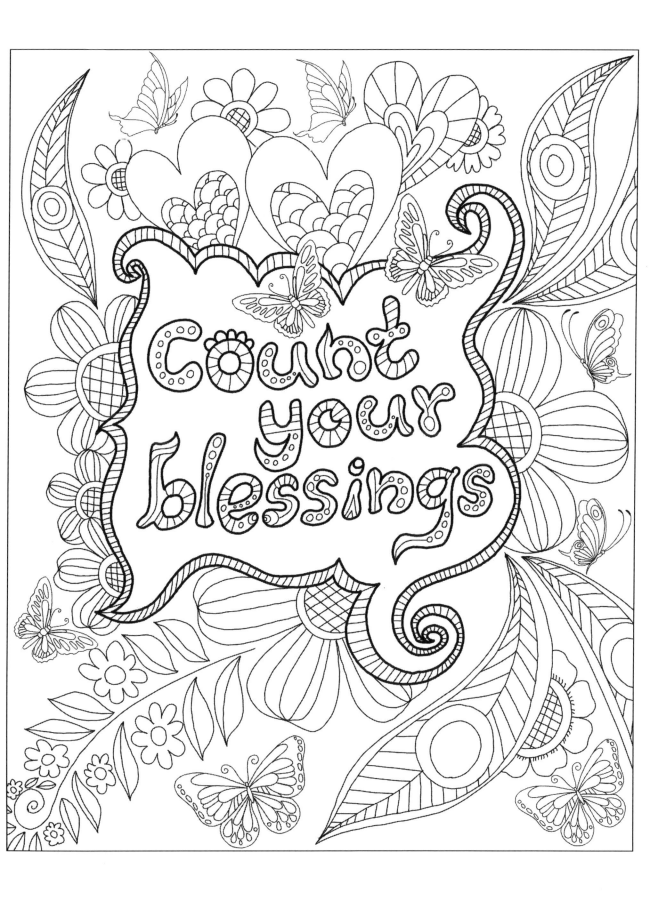

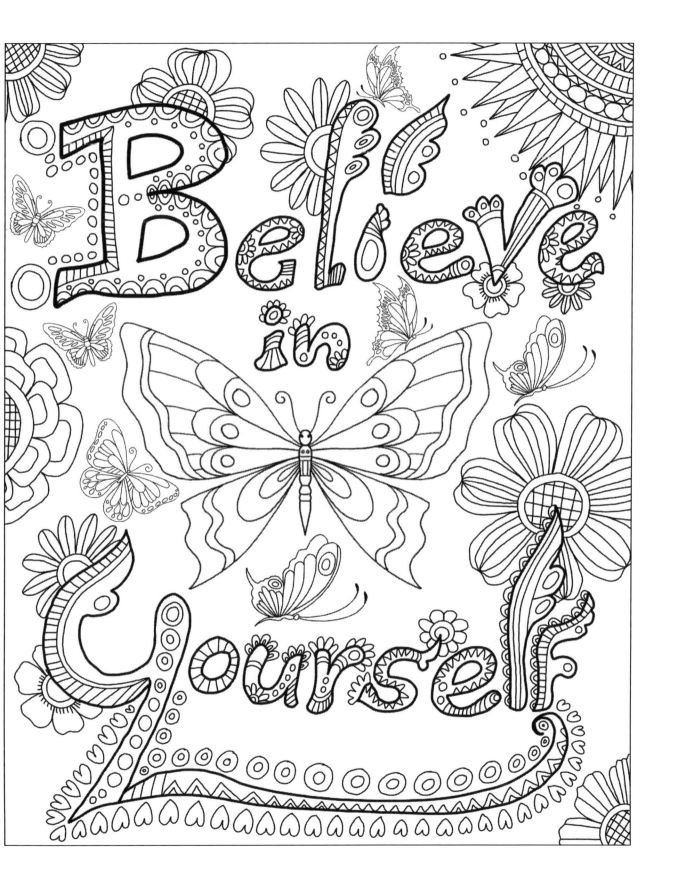

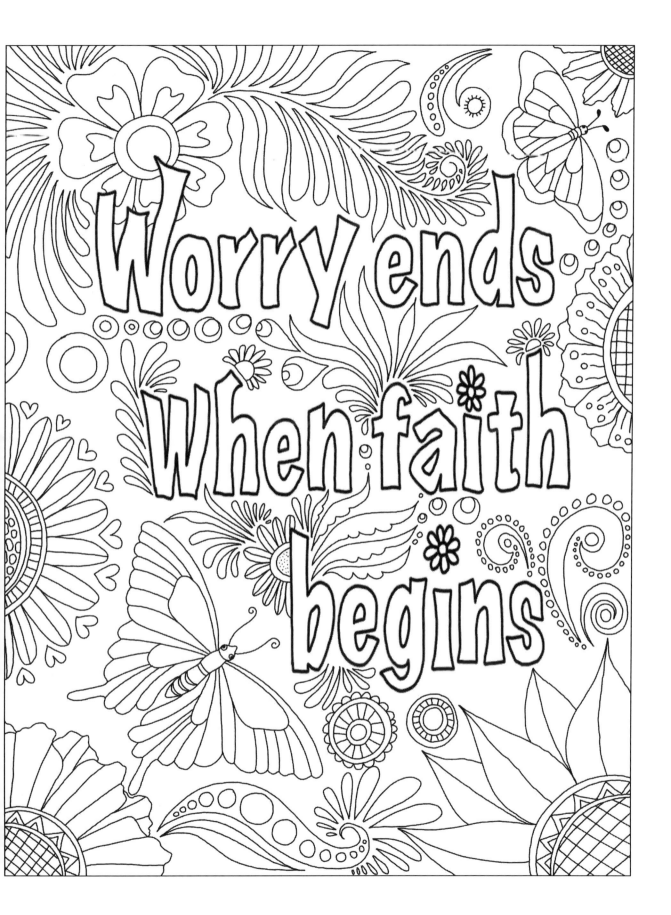

17778118R00038

Made in the USA
San Bernardino, CA
19 December 2018